A TRUE BOOK™

The Nervous System

CHRISTINE TAYLOR-BUTLER

Children's Press®
An Imprint of Scholastic Inc.
New York Toronto London Auckland Sydney
Mexico City New Delhi Hong Kong
Danbury, Connecticut

Content Consultant

Lawrence J. Cheskin, M.D., F.A.C.P.
Associate Professor of Medicine
Johns Hopkins University School of Medicine
Baltimore, Maryland

Library of Congress Cataloging-in-Publication Data

Taylor-Butler, Christine.
  The Nervous system / by Christine Taylor-Butler.
      p. cm. -- (A true book)
  Includes index.
    ISBN-13: 978-0-531-16861-5 (lib. bdg.)
              978-0-531-20735-2 (pbk.)
    ISBN-10: 0-531-16861-1 (lib. bdg.)
              0-531-20735-8 (pbk.)

1. Nervous system--Juvenile literature. I. Title. II. Series.

QP361.5.T39 2008
612.8--dc22   2007036015

Produced by Weldon Owen Education Inc.

©2008 Scholastic Inc.

1 2 3 4 5 6 7 8 9 10 R 17 16 15 14 13 12 11 10 09 08

Find the Truth!

Everything you are about to read is true *except* for one of the sentences on this page.

Which one is **TRUE**?

T or F You grow faster during the day than at night.

T or F The sound of a lawnmower can damage your hearing.

Find the answers in this book.

Contents

Without oxygen, brain cells start dying after about three minutes!

6

CHAPTER 1

Ouch!

You smell biscuits baking. Your mouth waters. The timer rings to signal that they are ready. When you look in the oven, you can see that they are golden brown. As they cool on the rack, you can't resist. You try to sneak one. Ouch! They're hot. You snatch your hand away in an instant. Your nervous system just protected you. But that is not all it did!

Touch is the only one of the senses that is located in all parts of your body.

One part of the nervous system works automatically.
It keeps you breathing even when you are sleeping.

What's Going On?

Your brain is a mass of nerves. It makes up the
control center for your body. Nerves in other parts
of your body tell the brain what is going on all
over the body. This system of nerves keeps all
other body systems operating. It does this even
when you are not thinking about it. For example,
it keeps your heart beating.

When you baked the biscuits, parts of your brain sent signals to your muscles. That set of signals allowed you to mix the dough, cut out the biscuits, and turn on the oven. Other parts of your nervous system worked without your control. Nerves in your nose sent information about the smell of the biscuit from the air to your brain. Nerves in your head made your mouth water. Nerves carried the message from your ears that the timer had gone off. Your eyes sent information about how delicious the biscuits looked.

Our sense of smell is responsible for about 80 percent of what we taste.

Most importantly, nerves in your fingertips told you that the biscuits were too hot. Your nerves told muscles in your arm to pull away quickly. This happened in a thousandth of a second. In fact, it happened before you could think about it. This protected you from getting a serious burn. A reaction like this is known as a **reflex** action.

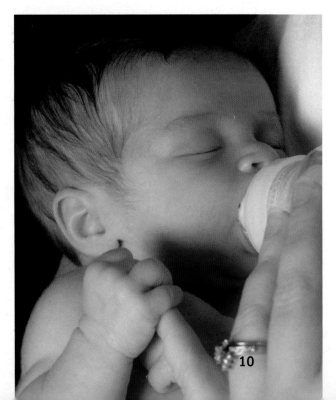

Newborn babies are born with the grasp reflex. They wrap their fingers automatically around anything that touches the palm of their hands.

Growing Pains

Did you know that you grow faster at night than you do during the day? Your growth rate is controlled by the **pituitary** (pih-TOO-uh-tehr-ee) gland. It sits at the base of your skull. Nerves in the brain control the pituitary gland. They tell it to release a hormone at night while you sleep. That's why you may wake up a tiny bit taller than the day before. When your bones and body grow, it may cause aches. These are known as growing pains.

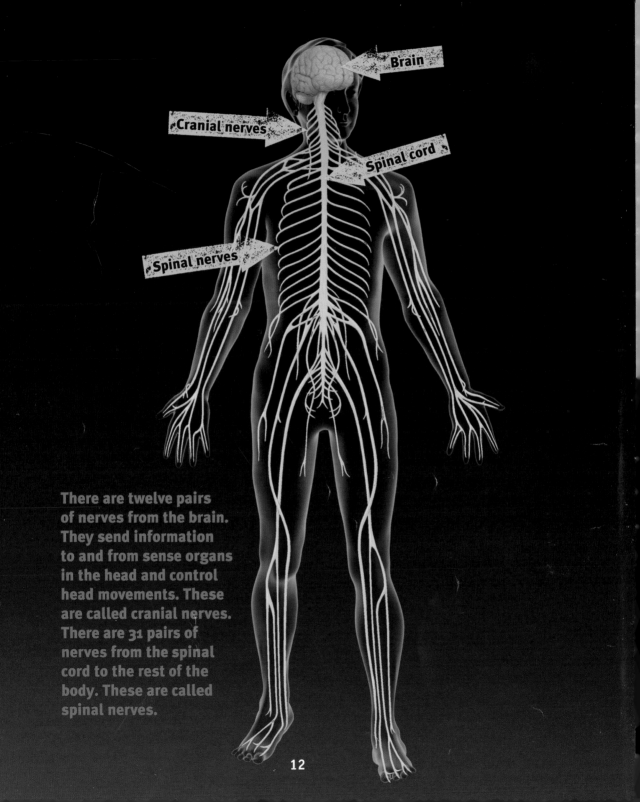

Brain

Cranial nerves

Spinal cord

Spinal nerves

There are twelve pairs of nerves from the brain. They send information to and from sense organs in the head and control head movements. These are called cranial nerves. There are 31 pairs of nerves from the spinal cord to the rest of the body. These are called spinal nerves.

CHAPTER 2

Information Highway

The nervous system consists of three main parts: the brain, the spinal cord, and the nerves that branch off from them. Think of the brain as being like a powerful computer. The spinal cord is like a thick cable of wires. It connects to the brain. The other nerves are the body's electrical wiring. They send signals to and from every part of the body.

Some nerve impulses travel faster than a Formula One race car!

The Control Center

The brain is made up of a huge network of nerves that are linked up. Signals travel along nerve pathways. The brain has many folds that increase its surface area. This way, lots of nerves can fit into a small space — the skull.

The brain has three main parts: the brain stem, the cerebrum (suh-REE-bruhm), and the cerebellum (sehr-uh-BEHL-uhm). The cerebrum is the largest part of the brain. It is the center of thinking. It controls memories and **voluntary** movements. The cerebellum is only one-eighth the size of your cerebrum. It controls things such as posture, balance, and coordination.

The cerebellum helps you learn actions that may seem difficult at first.

With practice, we can learn skills such as gymnastics. Eventually, we can do them almost automatically.

Main Parts of the Brain

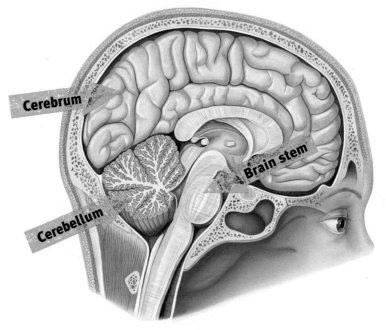

Cerebrum

Brain stem

Cerebellum

The brain stem connects the cerebrum to the spinal cord. It controls involuntary muscle movement. These are the actions of the body that happen even when you aren't thinking about them. Blinking or swallowing are examples of such actions. The brain stem controls things such as breathing and the heartbeat. It sorts messages from the body to the brain. It ensures that they go to the correct area of the brain.

The brain is divided into halves. These are called **hemispheres**. The left hemisphere controls the right side of the body. It is used mainly for rational thinking. The right hemisphere controls the left side of the body. It is used mainly for creative thinking. Each hemisphere is divided into four parts. These are called lobes.

The left side of the brain is strong in people who are good at math.

17

The Spinal Cord

The spinal cord is a thick, white tube of nerves.
It connects the brain to the nerves in the rest of
the body. It acts as a relay system for information
about what is going on inside your body. The nerves
in the spinal cord also control some processes
without input from the brain. For example,
they are responsible for reflexes. The spinal cord
is protected by a layer of spinal fluid and by
the backbone.

Parts of the Spine

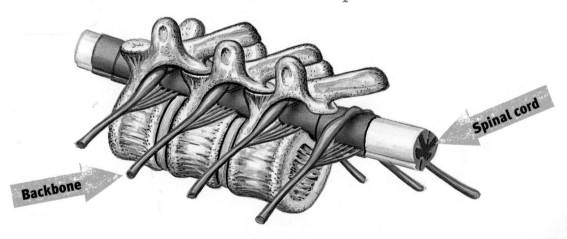

Spinal cord

Backbone

If the spinal cord is injured, signals may not be sent between the brain and the part of the body below the injury. As a result, that part of the body is paralyzed.

Scientists are working hard to find ways to help people who are **paralyzed**. They are experimenting with treatments to heal damaged nerves or make new ones grow. They are also developing computers to do the work of nerves. Some day, these computers may be capable of telling muscles to move.

The Body's Wiring

Nerves are made up of bundles of nerve cells, called neurons (NU-rons). Information travels along neurons in the form of electrical signals, or impulses. A neuron has three parts: dendrites, a cell body, and an axon. Dendrites receive impulses. Impulses then travel to the cell body. From the cell body, they travel the length of the axon to its end.

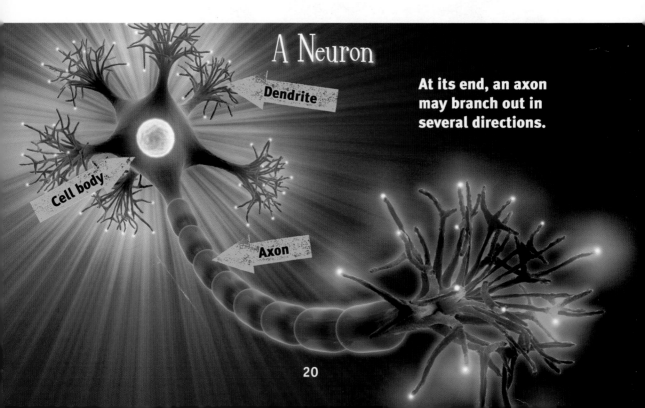

A Neuron

Dendrite

Cell body

Axon

At its end, an axon
may branch out in
several directions.

The Synapse: Where Two Neurons Meet

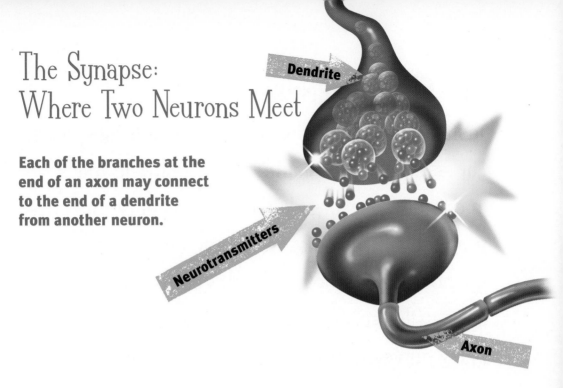

Dendrite

Neurotransmitters

Axon

Each of the branches at the end of an axon may connect to the end of a dendrite from another neuron.

There is a tiny gap between the end of an axon and the dendrite of another neuron. This gap is called a synapse (SIH-naps). To cross the gap, electrical signals change into chemical signals. The chemicals are called neurotransmitters. They flow across the synapse. Then they trigger an electrical signal in the dendrites of another neuron.

 Some neurons are as long as three feet (one meter).

The Chemical Senses

Taste and smell are known as the chemical senses. For taste, food **molecules** dissolve in the saliva in our mouths. For smell, molecules enter the nose from the air. They dissolve in the moist lining of the nose. There they come into contact with special cells, called receptors. These cells pass messages along nerves to the brain. Scientists think that we have hundreds of odor receptors. They think we have only about five kinds of taste receptors.

Time Line of Discovery

250 B.C. ➡
Greek scholar Aristotle believes that the nerves are controlled by the heart.

200 A.D. ➡
The Greek scientist Galen (GAY-luhn) discovers the role of the brain in the nervous system.

How come people can distinguish thousands of different tastes and odors? Taste and odor work together. Complex substances create thousands of different combinations of tastes and odors.

Before it goes anywhere else, the sense of smell connects to the part of the brain that controls emotions and memories. This is why smells often evoke strong memories.

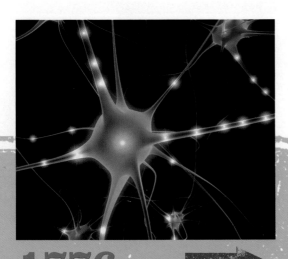

1776
Italian scientist Luigi Galvani discovers the electrical nature of nerve impulses.

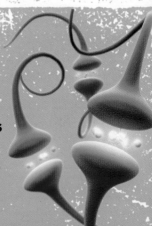

1998
Contrary to past belief, scientists discover that parts of the brain can form new neurons.

Scary Movie

When you watch a scary movie, your nervous system may respond as if there were a real danger or an emergency. This automatic reaction is known as the "fight or flight response." You are filled with extra energy and strength. In a real emergency, you are then ready to defend yourself (fight), or to escape (flight). This is the body's natural way of helping you survive. When there is no emergency, your nervous system directs energy back to normal bodily functions, such as digestion.

After Dark

Your nervous system senses that the music is getting spooky. Your heartbeat and breathing speed up,

Action Ready

Your muscles tense, ready for action. Your digestion slows down. More sugar is released into the blood. You

Yikes!

Your nervous system tells your eyes to close and your body to jump.

All Clear

The danger has passed. Your body goes back to normal. Your heartbeat and breathing slow down. Your muscles relax.

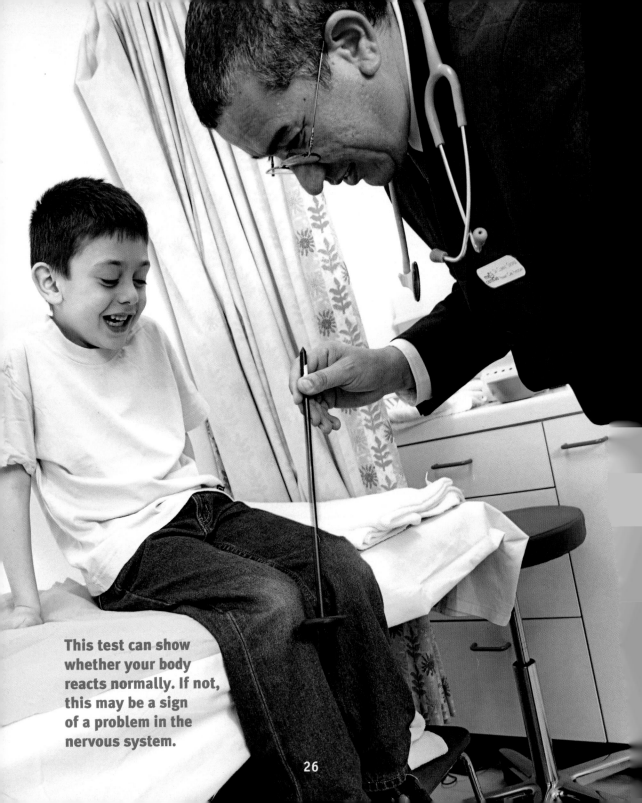

This test can show
whether your body
reacts normally. If not,
this may be a sign
of a problem in the
nervous system.

CHAPTER 3

A Gentle Tap

Checking that your nervous system is healthy is a normal part of a doctor's checkup. You may be asked to touch the tip of your nose without looking. The doctor may tap your elbow or shin with a small rubber reflex hammer. This tests your reflexes. Reflexes are bodily responses that happen without your having to think about them.

There are more than 2,500 touch receptors on a fingertip!

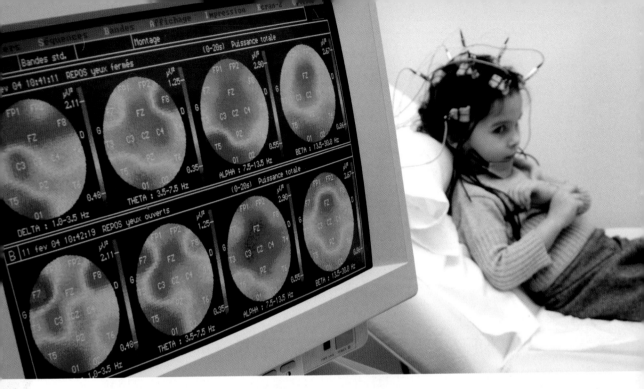

An EEG test is painless. A computer creates images that show the parts of the brain that are active as the patient reacts to different sights and sounds.

If anything appears to be wrong, more-complex tests can be done. Electroencephalography (ih-lehk-troh-en-sehf-uh-LOG-ruh-fee) measures the electrical impulses in the brain. This test is called an EEG for short. Electrodes on the head are connected to a machine by wires. The machine records the pattern of electrical impulses.

Sometimes a disease of the nervous system, such as a brain infection, can affect the fluid around the brain and spinal cord. To check for such a disease, doctors may take a sample of this fluid. To do this, doctors insert a needle into the spine. This procedure is called a spinal tap.

Ultrasound uses sound waves to make an image of a section of the body. Sound waves bounce off solid structures in your body. A computer turns the waves into an image. Doctors can use these images to check the brain and spinal cord.

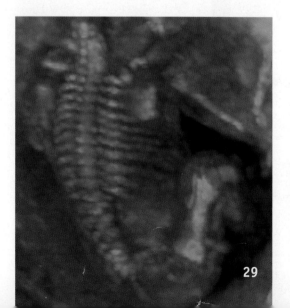

This ultrasound scan shows the spinal cord of an unborn baby.

A computerized axial tomography scan is also called a CAT, or CT, scan. It combines x-rays and computer technology. A CAT scan makes 3-D images of the inside of your body. Doctors can examine the body one "slice" at a time. This is useful for finding tumors or bleeding in the brain or spinal cord.

For a CAT scan, the patient lies on a table and is slid inside a huge cylinder.

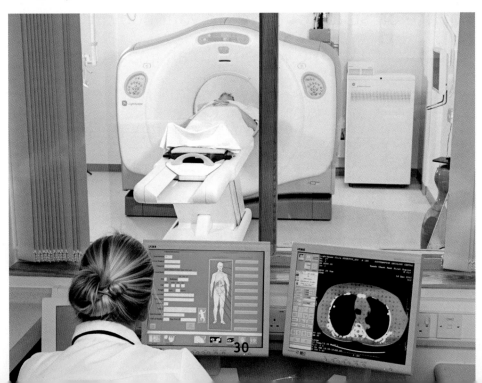

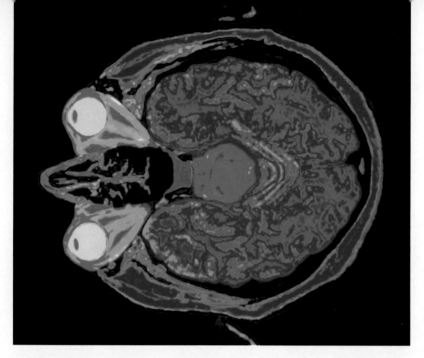

This MRI image shows a patient's brain, eyes, and, nose. A computer colors the different parts of the image so that they are easy to see.

A magnetic resonance imaging (MRI) machine is particularly good for examining soft tissues. It can see through bones. The patient is placed inside a very strong magnet. Then radio waves are sent through the body. The computer reads the signals sent out from the hydrogen atoms in the cells. MRI scans are even better than CTs for finding problems in the nervous system.

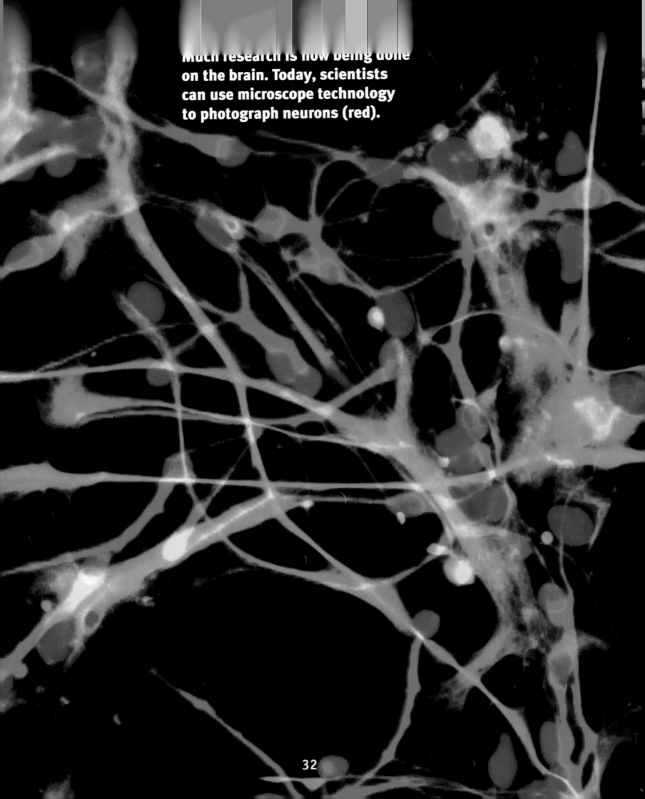

Much research is now being done on the brain. Today, scientists can use microscope technology to photograph neurons (red).

CHAPTER 4

When Signals Go Haywire

The nervous system is very complex. As with all parts of the body, illness or injury can damage it. The effects can be serious. However, every day, scientists are learning more about the nervous system. New treatments and medications are being developed constantly. There is new hope for many people suffering from nerve disorders.

 The human brain has about 100 billion neurons.

Too Many Signals

In epilepsy (EP-uh-lehp-see), there are sudden surges of abnormal electrical activity in the brain. These surges interrupt the way the brain functions. This causes **seizures**. At present, there is no cure for epilepsy. However, seizures are often controlled well with medication, diet, or surgery.

Chanda Gunn is an Olympic ice-hockey player. She has had epilepsy since she was nine years old.

Not Enough Signals

Cerebral (suh-REE-bruhl) palsy is caused by damage to the part of the brain that controls muscles and coordination. Some people are born with cerebral palsy. Some get it as a result of disease or injury. Cerebral palsy does not get worse over time. It varies from mild to severe. Early treatment is important. Many people with cerebral palsy can live independent, active lives.

Some people with cerebral palsy use crutches to help them walk. Service dogs can help with tasks such as opening doors.

Rerouting the Signals

Sounds travel as signals from the ear along a nerve to the brain. The signals do not travel through the spinal cord. The ears of some people who are deaf do not send sound messages to the nerves in their ears. **Cochlear** (KOKE-lee-ur) **implants** can help some of these people.

More than 20,000 people in the United States have cochlear implants. About half of these are children.

A cochlear implant has a microphone to pick up sound. This is worn behind the ear. A **speech processor** converts the sound into digital signals. It sends the digital signals to the implant under the skin. The implant sends electrical impulses to **electrodes** in the cochlea, in the inner ear. The electrodes stimulate the **auditory** nerve. The nerve sends signals to the brain.

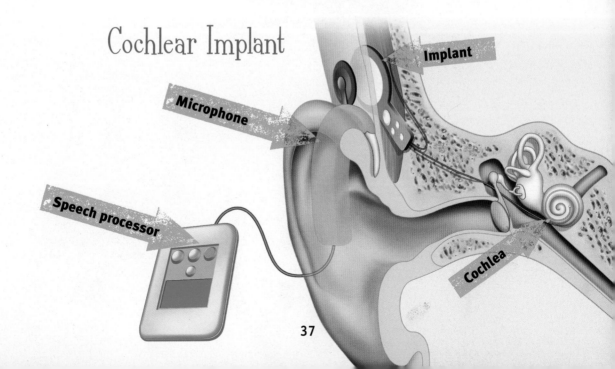

Cochlear Implant

Implant

Microphone

Speech processor

Cochlea

Always wear a helmet and other protective gear when doing sports such as biking, skating, or skateboarding.

CHAPTER 5

You've Got Nerve!

Wearing a helmet can reduce the risk of brain injury by as much as 80 percent.

There are billions of nerve cells in the human body. In 1998, scientists were surprised to find out that parts of the brain can grow new nerve cells. However, it seems that normally most of the brain and spinal cord cannot do this. Major injuries can lead to loss of some functions. So it is important to protect your nervous system from harm.

Protect Yourself

- Wear the right protective gear,
  such as a helmet, for the sports you play.
- Wear safety glasses when working on projects
  that may involve dust or debris.
- Wear a seatbelt whenever you are in a moving car.
- Wear a mask when exposed to strong fumes.
  Make sure there is plenty of fresh air in the room.
- Use earplugs around loud noises. Turn down loud
  music, especially when listening with headphones.
  Thousands of tiny hairs in your inner ear send
  signals to your auditory nerve. The hairs can
  break down if they are exposed to loud noise
  over a long a period of time. This can
  lead to permanent hearing loss.

Not So Loud!

Sounds louder than about 80 **decibels** (dB)
are considered harmful. Even softer sounds can
damage your ears if you listen for long periods
of time. Turn the sound down. Don't listen for
hours. Here's a sample of typical noise levels:

- 150 dB rock music at concert (extremely loud)
- 140 dB jet engine (extremely loud)
- 90 dB   lawnmower (loud)
- 50 dB   rainfall (medium)
- 30 dB   quiet library (soft)

In order to stay healthy, your nervous system needs the right vitamins and minerals. Eating a balanced diet can provide them.

Stay Healthy

Damage to the nervous system can also be caused by illness. You can help protect yourself by getting all your **immunizations**. Since your body makes spinal fluid every day, you need to drink plenty of water. The brain maintains a delicate and complex chemical balance. This keeps all systems in your body working properly. So it is smart not to take in any substances that could disturb that balance. ★

Approximate number of neurons in the brain:
100 billion

Approximate number of synapses in the body:
About one quadrillion

Average weight of the brain: About 3 lb (1.4 kg)

Surface area of the brain: About 230 to 470 sq in (1,500 to 3,000 sq cm)

Average length of the spinal cord: About 18 in (45 cm)

Average number of taste buds: About 10,000

Longest and thickest nerve in the body:
Sciatic nerve

First sense to develop: Touch

Did you find the truth?

F You grow faster during the day than at night.

T The sound of a lawnmower can damage your hearing.

Resources

Books

Ballard, Carol. *The Brain and Nervous System*. Detroit: KidHaven Press, 2005.

DK Publishing. *Alive: The Living Breathing Human Body Book*. New York: DK Children, 2007.

Houghton, Gillian. *Nerves: The Nervous System*. New York: Powerkids Press, 2007.

Jakab, Cheryl. *Nervous System*. Mankato, MN: Smart Apple Media, 2007.

Parker, Steve. *Control Freak: Hormones, the Brain, and the Nervous System*. Chicago: Raintree, 2006.

Petrie, Kristin. *The Nervous System*. Edina, MN: Checkerboard Books, 2006.

Royston, Angela. *Why Do I Get Toothache?: And Other Questions About Nerves*. Portsmouth, NH: Heinemann Library, 2003.

Silverman, Buffy. *Who's in Control?: Brain and Nervous System*. Chicago: Raintree, 2006.

Stangl, Jean. *What Makes You Cough, Sneeze, Burp, Hiccup, Blink, Yawn, Sweat, and Shiver* (My Health). New York: Franklin Watts, 2000.

Organizations and Web Sites

Get Body Smart
www.getbodysmart.com/ap/nervoussystem/menu/
menu.html
View animations and take quizzes on the nervous system.

National Science Teachers Association:
Nervous System Guide
www.nsta.org/publications/interactive/nerves
Explore nerve cells up close with animated diagrams.

Neuroscience For Kids
http://faculty.washington.edu/chudler/introb.html
Study in-depth information, experiments, and the latest news.

Place to Visit

Science Museum of Virginia
2500 West Broad Street
Richmond, VA
804-864-1400
www.smv.org/nowshowing/
exhibitions/bioscape.asp
Test your reflexes and senses
in the My Size Gallery.

Important Words

auditory (AW-dih-tor-ee) – having to do with hearing

cochlear (KOKE-lee-ur) **implant** – a device that helps some people who are deaf hear sounds

decibel (DESS-uh-bel) – a unit for measuring the volume of sounds

electrode – a part on an electronic device where electric current can be discharged from the device into the body

hemisphere (HEM-uhs-feer) – half of a sphere

immunization (im-yu-nih-ZAY-shuhn) – an injection or dose of vaccine that protects against a particular disease

molecule (MOL-uh-kyool) – the smallest part of a substance that displays all the properties of that substance

paralyzed – having nerve damage that hinders use of part of the body

pituitary (pih-TOO-uh-tehr-ee) – a gland that produces various hormones and releases them into the bloodstream

reflex – an automatic action that happens without a person's control or effort

seizure (SEE-zhur) – a sudden, uncontrolled muscle spasm

speech processor – a computerized device that converts sounds into digital signals

voluntary – controlled by the will

Index

About the Author

Christine Taylor-Butler lives in Kansas City, Missouri, with her husband and two daughters. A native of Ohio, she is the author of more than 40 books for children. She holds a B.S. degree in both Civil Engineering and Art and Design from the Massachusetts Institute of Technology in Cambridge, MA. Other books by Ms. Taylor-Butler in the True Book Health and the Human Body series include: *The Food Pyramid*, *Food Allergies*, *Food Safety*, *The Circulatory System*, *The Digestive System*, and *The Respiratory System*.

PHOTOGRAPHS: Anne Luo/Weldon Owen Education (p. 12; neurons, p. 23); BAA Aviation Photo Library (p. 41); Banana Stock/Soul Child (p. 8); Courtesy of Woodward West (p. 38); Getty Images (p. 24; p. 32; p. 34); iStockPhoto.com (back cover; p. 3; skull, p. 4; scone, p. 9; p. 10; p. 13; Aristotle, p. 22; ear plugs, p. 40; © Kiyoshi Takahase Segundo, p. 20 and brain, p. 22; © Sebastian Kaulitzki, nerve impulses, p. 23); Photodisc (p. 17); Photolibrary (cover; p. 26; pp. 28–31); Stock.XCHNG (p. 27); Stockxpert (p. 43); Tranz: Corbis (p. 6; p. 11; p. 15; p. 19; p. 35; p. 42); Reuters (p. 36). All other images property of Weldon Owen Education.